The Disease Fighters

The Disease Fighters

The Nobel Prize in Medicine

by Nathan Aaseng

Lerner Publications Company • Minneapolis

To Sharla

The glossary on page 75 gives definitions for
the words in bold face type.

LIBRARY OF CONGRESS CATALOGING-IN-PUBLICATION DATA

Aaseng, Nathan.
   The disease fighters.

   (Nobel Prize winners)
   Includes index.
   Summary: Describes some of the major medical discoveries, such as the cure for tuberculosis and the
cause of malaria, made by researchers who were eventually
awarded the Nobel Prize for Medicine.
   1. Medicine—Awards. 2. Nobel prizes. [1. Nobel
prizes. 2. Medical research. 3. Physicians.
4. Scientists.] I. Title. II. Series.
R699.A27   1987   610'.79   87-2903
ISBN 0-8225-0652-1 (lib. bdg.)

Manufactured in the United States of America

   2   3   4   5   6   7   8   9   10 96 95 94 93 92 91 90 89 88

Contents

French chemist Louis Pasteur laid the groundwork for countless Nobel Prize-winning medical discoveries.

Introduction

How often have you heard someone say, "It's only a sore throat," or, "It's just a cut, nothing to worry about," and thought little of it? Medicine has come so far that it's easy to forget the danger that used to lie behind these minor complaints.

Throughout most of history, parents had to fight off panic when their children didn't feel well. A simple sore throat could be an early sign of diphtheria, a disease that once killed thousands of people, especially children, each year. A small scratch or a cut could not be forgotten once it was cleaned and bandaged, for it could lead to a deadly infection. Cuts and sore throats weren't the only dangers. People also had to watch out for mosquito bites, crowded beaches, and hundreds of other hazards that could lead to incurable diseases.

Until very recently, people had nowhere to turn for help when they were sick. They could see a doctor, but doctors could usually do little more than prescribe something to ease their suffering. If there was a "cure" available, it was sometimes worse than the disease. Perhaps the most hopeless option was to go to the hospital. If people weren't mortally ill when they were admitted, a short stay in the hospital was often enough for them to catch a deadly contagious disease.

The Threat to Civilization

A brief look at nearly any era in history is all that is needed to illustrate the enormous advances that have been made in medicine. When remembering past catastrophes that have taken many lives, people tend to focus on the more dramatic events such as great battles and natural disasters. But the truth is that erupting volcanoes and flying bullets have killed far fewer people than humanity's greatest enemy: disease.

Disease has struck without warning countless times in the past, burying the most dominant societies on earth. The disease that has done the most damage is probably the bubonic plague. In 430 B.C., the great Athenian Empire crumbled because of the devastation brought on by the plague, and another outbreak of the disease in Rome in A.D. 262 is said to have killed 5,000 people each day. The bubonic plague visited Europe several times during the Middle Ages. Estimates of the numbers left dead in the wake of the epidemic of 1348 range from one-fourth to three-fourths of the entire population of Europe!

Those who went off to war in the Middle Ages rarely survived long enough even to see the enemy. Of the estimated 500,000 Christian warriors who joined the Crusades—the expedition to capture the Holy Land from the Muslims—only about 20,000 avoided illness long enough to make it to their destination. As late as 1870, disease continued to claim the lives of from 4 to 10 times as many soldiers as did combat. The Russo-Japanese War at the beginning of the 20th century is believed to be the first major war in which battle wounds killed more soldiers than disease.

Travel to foreign lands was once very dangerous, not only for explorers, but also for natives who encountered foreigners. It was not the might and cunning of the Spanish that destroyed the powerful empires of the Aztecs and the Mayas, but the smallpox and scarlet fever that the Europeans accidentally introduced when they landed in Mexico. When exploration parties probed the interior of the African continent, they encountered new diseases as well as new lands and were often wiped out.

People were nearly powerless against the ravages of these diseases. Groping for remedies, they lit fires to purify the air and sealed "poisoned" wells, which were supposedly the source of the evil. They bled the sick and took them to kings to be healed by a monarch's magic touch. Over a million frightened people undertook a mass pilgrimage to Rome one year, hoping somehow to escape disease, and 9 out of 10 of the pilgrims died on the way. Up until the mid-1800s, medicine was unable to improve on an average life expectancy of about 35 years for the well-to-do and even less for commoners.

Gift of Life

The breakthrough into the modern age of medicine came in the last half of the 19th century when Louis Pasteur suggested what many cultures had suspected for years, that disease can be caused by organisms too small to be seen by the naked eye. Scientists were soon hot on the trail of these tiny killers, and before the turn of the century, they had found the microorganisms responsible for such deadly diseases as tuberculosis, diphtheria, and malaria. Others built on the work of these pioneers in microbiology and discovered cures for diseases that had puzzled doctors for centuries.

Some of the most dramatic changes in the ways we prevent and treat disease have been brought about by scientists whose achievements were rewarded with

The Nobel Prize for physiology or medicine. Alfred Nobel is pictured on the front, and on the back the Genius of Medicine is shown drawing water for a sick girl.

the Nobel Prize for physiology or medicine. This prize was one of five such honors set up by Swedish millionaire Alfred Nobel at the end of the 19th century. A chemist who had grown rich through his invention of a powerful destructive force, dynamite, the conscience-stricken Nobel decided to use his vast fortune to make the world a better place. In his will, he set aside a great share of his estate to fund the Nobel Prizes, five awards that would be given each year to those who had done the most to benefit humanity in the areas of peace, literature, physics, chemistry, and physiology or medicine.

Evidence of the triumph over disease can be seen in countries all over the world. In 1900, infectious diseases were the top three causes of death in the United States, but by 1954, the death rate from all infectious diseases in the United States was down more than 90 percent. Thanks

in part to the prizewinners in this book, it is not uncommon today for people to live to be 70, 80, or even 90 years old.

The greatest blessing given to the world by the Nobel Prize-winning researchers, however, was the gift of life to children. The deadly diseases that they studied had done the greatest damage to the very young. Before the 17th century, parents could expect that three of every four children born to them would die in infancy. Even as late as 1900, 30 percent of the children in the United States died before they reached adolescence. Most of them would have lived had their doctors had the knowledge that has since been given to us by Nobel Prize winners. Of all the people who have worked for the good of humanity, none can point to more concrete evidence of their success than those who have earned the Nobel Prize for their work in medicine.

1

The White Death

For hundreds of years, the world was ravaged by a disease with an ominous name—the white death. By the time of the American Revolution, this disease was the most common cause of death in the Western world, and the prospects were not much better 100 years later when it still claimed the life of 1 out of every 500 Americans annually. Although it is no longer the threat it once was, most people are still familiar with the white death. Today we call this disease tuberculosis.

Tuberculosis was known as the white death because as the disease progressed, its victims lost their color and pale grayish lumps called **tubercles** formed throughout the inside of their bodies. One of its other nicknames, which appeared often in the literature of the 18th and 19th centuries, was consumption, a term that described how tuberculosis

seemed to eat slowly at its victims' flesh and vitality until it finally killed them. The more acute cases were referred to as galloping consumption.

Until the last part of the 19th century, people could only speculate about the cause of tuberculosis. Because it seemed to be primarily a poor person's disease, tuberculosis was often blamed on nutritional shortages. This theory, however, did not explain how someone as privileged as Napoleon II, the son of a French emperor, could come down with the disease. Some guessed that tuberculosis

Once it was discovered that microorganisms can cause disease, hospital workers began to wear masks and gowns and were careful to sterilize anything that might have come in contact with disease-causing microorganisms.

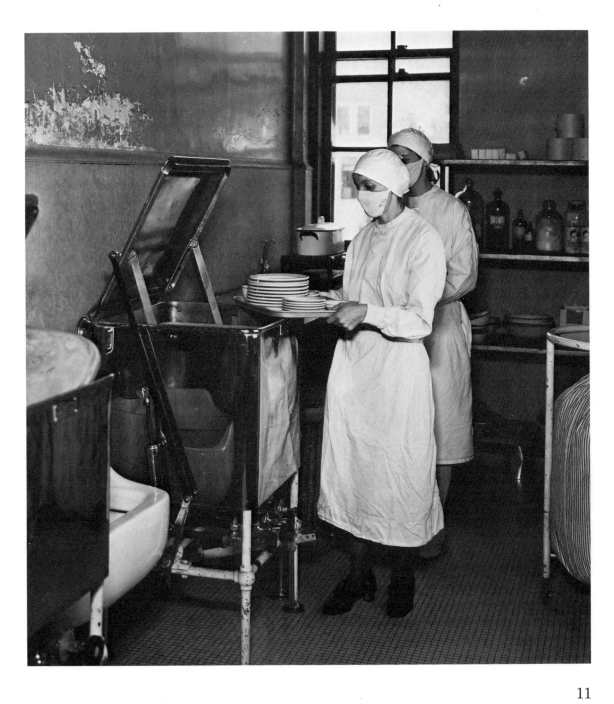

was basically an emotional disorder, while others thought that an inherited weakness made some people prone to the disease.

The one thing that was certain about tuberculosis was that it was very contagious. There are several forms of the illness, each affecting a different part of the body such as the glands or the skin, but the worst kind takes hold in the lungs. Victims of this form cough a great deal and can pass on the disease through the air to anyone who gets near them. For this reason, tuberculosis victims—even famous ones—were once shunned by society. While traveling, the great pianist and composer Frederic Chopin was coldly kicked out of his lodgings onto the street when it was discovered he suffered from consumption.

Lack of knowledge about the cause of the white death led to some strange attempts at cures. As late as the 1800s, treatments for tuberculosis were still based on nothing more than wild, and

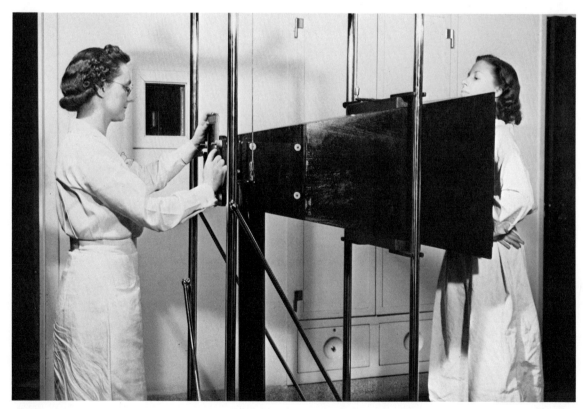

In the 1930s, X rays were commonly used to detect tuberculosis.

Robert Koch

Laying the Groundwork

Some of the greatest contributions to the medical knowledge of the late 19th century were made by a man from Klausthal, Germany, who had been groomed by his father to be a shoemaker. Fortunately this man, whose name was Robert Koch, had greater ambitions for himself. He decided to study medicine and eventually settled down as a country doctor and district medical officer in the small town of Posen in Prussia.

After practicing medicine for several years, Koch slumped into despair because of the helplessness of his profession. People came to him desperate for cures, yet there were so few remedies he could offer that would do any good. Koch actually preferred research in natural science to the practice of medicine, so to cheer him up, his wife bought him a microscope for his 28th birthday. From that time on, Koch saved precious moments each day to explore the world beyond the reach of human vision. He was especially intrigued by the tiny one-celled organisms called **bacteria** that seemed to be everywhere.

Koch was not the first researcher to see bacteria. That honor goes to Dutchman Anton van Leeuwenhoek, an amateur scientist who discovered the existence of bacteria and other **microorganisms** in the 1670s. After their discovery, very little was learned about the tiny organisms that Leeuwenhoek had seen through his

sometimes foolish, guesses. Many people believed that the kings of England and France had special healing powers and that a touch from one of them could cure the disease. Others were told that regular drinks of cognac would do the trick. The truth was that very little could be done about tuberculosis or any of the other terrible diseases that plagued the world until some important medical groundwork had been laid.

13

microscope until they caught the attention of scientists like Louis Pasteur and Robert Koch almost two hundred years later.

In the mid-1800s, while doing research for the French wine industry, Louis Pasteur came to the startling conclusion that some diseases are caused by microorganisms. Although many doctors refused to believe the French chemist's theory, some—including a district medical officer in Prussia—took Pasteur's claims very seriously.

During the course of his research, Koch noticed that there were tiny rod-shaped bacteria growing in the blood of sheep infected with a disease called anthrax. He was, however, unable to find these rods in blood drawn from healthy sheep. Guessing that the bacteria must have something to do with the disease, Koch injected bacteria-laden blood from a sheep with anthrax into a healthy mouse. As he had expected, the mouse developed anthrax and died. When he injected blood from the first mouse into a second mouse, the second animal also died of the disease. Every time one of

In this cartoon from 1897, an early bacteriologist studies a mischievous "microorganism."

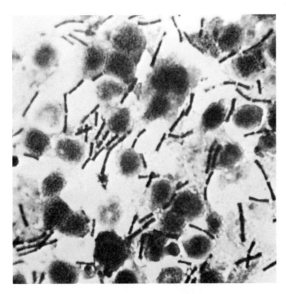

The rod-shaped organisms scattered throughout this blood specimen are anthrax bacteria.

In 1876, Robert Koch announced that he had proven Pasteur's theory that a disease could be caused by one specific microorganism. The medical world was still skeptical, but Koch was a meticulous scientist whose methods of research in **microbiology** were far ahead of those used by most of his peers, and there was no way anyone could argue with the results of his experiments. World-famous microbiologists had to agree with the findings of the country doctor.

While studying the anthrax bacterium, Koch also set down the following four rules of disease research, which scientists in every respected laboratory have learned to follow when working with bacteria.

1. A specific organism must be associated with all cases of the disease.
2. A pure culture of this organism must be isolated and grown outside of the body.
3. The culture that has been grown must cause the disease whenever it is injected into a healthy animal.
4. The organism must be isolated from the diseased animal and grown again.

his test animals developed anthrax, Koch found the rod-shaped bacteria in its bloodstream.

Koch knew that he was on the verge of an important discovery. Before he could announce his findings, however, he had to be sure that it was the bacterium itself, not something else that might have gotten into his specimens, that was causing the disease. In order to do this, Koch invented a slide that enabled him to grow pure, or uncontaminated, **cultures** of the bacteria while observing them under a microscope. When Koch injected a test animal with the bacteria, it soon developed anthrax. He had his proof that the rod-shaped bacteria caused anthrax.

Accidental Progress

Koch was rewarded for his discovery with a job in the laboratories of the Imperial Health Office in Berlin, a great change from his makeshift laboratory in Posen. While his research methods were being

15

picked up by scientists in pursuit of a wide range of diseases, Koch decided to tackle the most serious illness of his time, tuberculosis.

The experiment that helped Koch pin down the tuberculosis bacterium was not only an accident, it was an outright mistake. While Koch was looking for a dye that would make microorganisms in tuberculosis tissue show up under a microscope, he carelessly left a slide sitting in a blue dye for several hours. When he discovered his oversight, Koch assumed that the long period of exposure must surely have ruined the experiment, and he nearly threw the slide away. But upon examining it under a microscope, he found that the old dye had made thin, curved rods appear in the tuberculosis tissue. When Koch examined the tubercles of animals that had died from tuberculosis, he found them to be full of the bacteria. In 1882, Koch announced that he had found the tuberculosis bacterium.

Tuberculosis research was helped along once again by another mistake, this time made by Koch's fellow scientist Paul Ehrlich. Ehrlich left a slide of the hard-to-detect bacteria on a stove, not realizing that a conscientious housekeeper would get to the laboratory before him the next day and light the stove to warm up the room. Instead of ruining his slide, however, the heat made the bacteria even easier to see.

Once he had the tools to make tuberculosis bacteria visible, Koch set out to

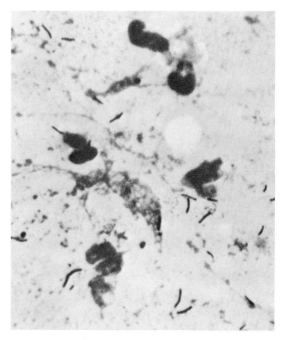

Tuberculosis bacteria show up as curved rods in this sputum sample from a tuberculosis victim.

find a cure for the disease. He had trouble growing the deadly bacteria in the laboratory until he discovered that it would thrive in animal blood. Once he had built up enough of the bacteria, Koch began to use it in experiments with hundreds of mice, rats, chickens, cats, and dogs. After years of study, Robert Koch thrilled the world in 1890 with the announcement that he had developed a cure for tuberculosis. He claimed that tuberculin, an extract obtained from dead bacteria taken from tubercles, could cure the disease.

Unfortunately, a quick cure for the white

death was not to be found. The great hope kindled by tuberculin was doused when it was determined that Koch's remedy didn't work. Despite this setback, Koch's work was not in vain. Others continued the fight against tuberculosis where he had left off, and eventually several drugs were developed that would stop the growth of the tuberculosis bacterium. Scientists were even able to find a purpose for tuberculin, which is now used as a tool in the early detection of tuberculosis.

The Nobel committee recognized Koch's contribution to the study of tuberculosis by awarding him the 1905 Nobel Prize for physiology or medicine. Perhaps even more important than Koch's work with tuberculosis, however, were the advances he made in the study of bacteria, which made it possible for scientists to do battle against countless other diseases.

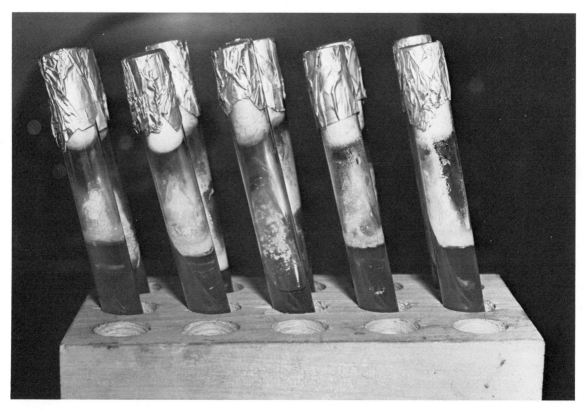

Scientists often use animal blood to grow tuberculosis bacteria for study. These test tubes contain tuberculosis bacteria from cows.

2

The Choking Death

You probably remember going to the doctor for a diphtheria-tetanus shot, and chances are you don't look forward to getting another. Injections like this might not seem so bad, however, if you knew something about the diseases that they prevent.

Although diphtheria—one of the diseases prevented by diphtheria-tetanus shots—is an ancient disease, people didn't even know it existed until the 18th century. Before then, those who had diphtheria were thought to be suffering from some other throat condition such as scarlet fever. During the 18th and 19th centuries, the Industrial Revolution in Europe and North America brought scores of people into the cities, and crowded living conditions led to a dramatic increase in contagious diseases. Of these

diseases, diphtheria was especially brutal because of its fatality rate—sometimes as high as 90 percent—and because it so often struck children.

The word *diphtheria* comes from a Greek word meaning "leather," which refers to the tough, leathery membrane that forms in the throats of its victims. Other symptoms include a sore throat, a fever, and swollen lymph nodes. Deaths from the disease usually occurred when the throat membranes became so thick that they blocked the breathing passages, which led to diphtheria's common name,

Dr. Béla Schick tests school children for susceptibility to diphtheria by injecting them with diphtheria bacteria. This procedure, which Schick pioneered, is called the Schick test.

18

19

Edward Jenner

the choking death. The deadly disease could strike very fast. George Washington, one of the more famous people believed to have fallen victim to diphtheria, first complained of a pain in his throat on December 13, 1799, and within 48 hours he was dead.

Behring and Antitoxin

As was true with tuberculosis, several medical developments led up to the mastery of diphtheria. In the 1790s, English physician Edward Jenner discovered that he could protect people from smallpox by infecting them with cowpox, a mild disease related to smallpox. Once they had recovered from cowpox, they were **immune** to the more serious disease. It was years before scientists could see

Diphtheria was such a dangerous illness that its victims and their families had to be quarantined so they wouldn't spread the disease.

This cartoon showing Jenner infecting people with cowpox to protect them against smallpox makes fun of people's fear that the vaccine would turn them into cows.

a way to apply Jenner's discovery to anything except smallpox because other diseases did not have related illnesses that would provide immunity.

Then, in the 1880s, Louis Pasteur found that if he injected a test animal with a solution of disease-causing microorganisms that had been weakened, later called a **vaccine**, the animal would become mildly ill but once recovered would be immune to that same disease. This method of **immunization** is called **vaccination**. Vaccines stimulate the body to produce **antibodies**, substances that fight disease.

Robert Koch's discovery that a disease can be caused by a specific kind of bacterium led to a massive hunt for these tiny villains, and in 1883, pathologist Edwin Klebs isolated the bacteria responsible for diphtheria. A few years later, it was found that the symptoms of diphtheria were not caused by the bacterium itself, but rather by a **toxin**, or poison, produced by the bacterium.

That was as far as the science of medicine had advanced regarding diphtheria when Emil von Behring turned his attention to the disease. Behring, born in West Prussia in 1854, received medical training as a military surgeon in the German army. In 1889, he joined the world-famous laboratories of bacteriologist Robert Koch as an assistant.

That same year, an important discovery was made in the Koch laboratories. A Japanese bacteriologist named Shibasaburo Kitasato discovered the bacterium that causes tetanus. Tetanus is a paralyzing disease that is sometimes called lockjaw because it contracts the muscles so tightly that some victims are unable to open their mouths. Scientists soon discovered that, like diphtheria, the lethal symptoms of tetanus were brought on by a toxin manufactured by the tetanus bacterium. With this information, Behring and Kitasato decided to work together to try and set up an immunization program for tetanus based on the work of Jenner and Pasteur.

Since the toxin was responsible for the damage to tetanus victims, Behring and Kitasato concentrated on creating an immunity to this substance rather than to tetanus bacteria. They began their experiments by injecting a small amount of tetanus toxin into test animals. The animals immediately began to develop antibodies to protect themselves from the poison and were able to withstand a larger dose of toxin the next time. The scientists gradually increased the amount of toxin until the animals were immune to the disease.

Emil von Behring

As part of their experiments, Behring and Kitasato took **serum**—the liquid part of the blood that is left when the blood clots—from the immune animals and injected it into a second group of test animals. When they tried to infect the second group with tetanus, not one of the animals developed the disease. Apparently, the serum contained antibodies that could be used to protect other animals from tetanus. These antibodies are called **antitoxins**.

22

When Behring took up the more urgent task of dealing with diphtheria, he at first ignored his previous work with antitoxins and tried to use chemicals to kill the bacterial invader that caused the disease. But all Behring succeeded in doing was killing off a large supply of guinea pigs. Although the chemicals proved useless in combating diphtheria, there were occasionally some guinea pigs that were able to survive the disease on their own. When Behring tested these, he found that they had become immune to further efforts to inflict the disease on them. So much for chemical cures; Behring was back on the antitoxin trail. It wasn't long before he announced that serum taken from immune guinea pigs contained an antitoxin that would protect against diphtheria.

A Special Christmas

Behring's discovery was greeted with excitement by the medical world.

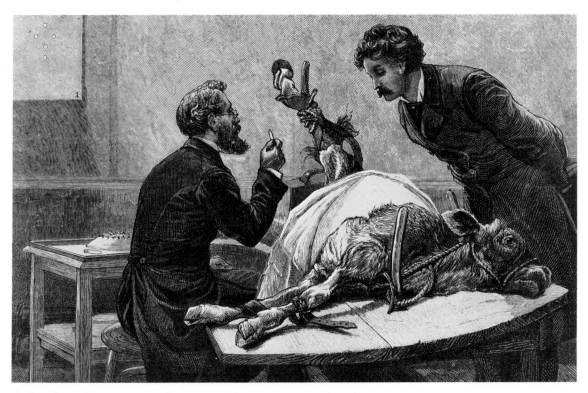

Scientists draw serum from a calf to use as antitoxin.

A researcher makes antitoxin in his laboratory at the Pasteur Institute in 1895.

Although the diphtheria antitoxin had only been tried on animals, there was the obvious possibility that it could be used to immunize humans. Unfortunately, this hope was squelched when Behring discovered that the immunity provided by an injection of antitoxin lasted only about 10 days. There was no way that immunization would be practical if the process had to be repeated every 10th day. There was, however, a chance that the antitoxin could help those who already had diphtheria battle the deadly disease. Behring went to work turning dogs and sheep into small antitoxin factories in order to produce enough serum for use with humans.

The first chance to try this cure on a human came on Christmas night, 1891, in Berlin, Germany, where a child was deathly ill with diphtheria. A dose of Behring's antitoxin was injected into the child, and then everyone waited anxiously to see what would happen. The child recovered so quickly that it seemed nothing short of a miracle. For the first time, humans had concocted a remedy to stop a disease that already had a victim in its death grip. Moreover, since the antitoxin research had been relatively straightforward, it seemed that the medical profession was on the verge of a breakthrough that would quickly wipe out a host of diseases.

Dealing with Dosage

The excitement over the Christmas miracle was short-lived. Behring had been lucky with that first patient; in the cases that followed, some people were saved, but many died. The problem was that there was no way of knowing how much antitoxin was enough to do the job. Doctors needed a way of gauging the strength of the substance and of tailoring it to each individual patient.

That brought another German scientist, Paul Ehrlich, into the picture. Ehrlich fought successful battles against a number of diseases, including tuberculosis and syphilis. Born in 1854 in what is now Poland, Ehrlich had the kind of brilliantly inventive mind that caused him problems in a standard classroom but forged breakthroughs in the laboratory. It was he who defined many of the terms we now use in the field of **immunology**.

Ehrlich was able to work out an exact mathematical guide for determining the strength of bacterial toxins and antitoxins and for standardizing the doses to be used in combating disease. He also stepped up production of diphtheria antitoxins by producing antitoxin with horses, which have more blood—and,

therefore, more blood serum—than the animals that had been used before.

Ehrlich's work made antitoxins both practical and reliable, and within 10 years, the death rate for all types of diphtheria had declined dramatically. In 1894, London health officials had reported that 62 percent of those who contracted the disease died from it, and by 1910, that figure had dwindled to 12 percent. Diphtheria, which was one of the leading causes of death in the United States at the turn of the century, quickly dropped off the mortality charts. Years later, through the work of several scientists, it became possible not only to cure the disease, but also to vaccinate against it. Today the choking disease, while not completely eliminated, is no longer a major health problem.

For his pioneering efforts in this triumph, Emil von Behring was awarded the first Nobel Prize for physiology or medicine, presented to him in 1901. Paul Ehrlich received his Nobel Prize in 1908 in honor of his work in the field of immunology.

3

Magic Bullets

The future for medicine looked bright as the world entered the 20th century. Recent medical breakthroughs in the areas of vaccination, or vaccine therapy, and antitoxins, or serotherapy, had made it possible for doctors to save patients from terrible diseases that were once thought to be incurable. There were still, however, far more diseases that didn't respond to any known treatment.

The fight against these diseases was taken up by a scientist named Paul Ehrlich with a new weapon called **chemotherapy**. It was Ehrlich's dream to find, somewhere in nature or in a laboratory, a "magic

Paul Ehrlich searches for a "magic bullet" to use against disease.

bullet," a drug composed of chemicals that would zero in on the microorganisms that cause disease and destroy them without harming the patient. In the first half of the 20th century, Ehrlich and many others conducted a massive search for that magic bullet, starting with the disease syphilis.

The Romantic Killer

It is hard to believe that a sickness that has caused millions of deaths over the years could have been treated as a status symbol. But this was the case with syphilis, which was known for a time in Europe as the "malady of love" because it spread through sexual contact. The

27

disease was considered in many circles to be a mark of an adventurer and even good experience for a young man. People didn't take syphilis seriously because it progressed in several stages, and many never saw how bad it could be. Once the initial sores had disappeared, it seemed as though the patient had been cured. After a period of 3 to 10 years or even longer, however, syphilis entered its final stage, which could cause disfigurement, madness, and death.

Although there was no cure for the disease, syphilis victims who could afford treatment were subjected to painful, sometimes even dangerous treatments. The most popular remedy was the sweat stove. Patients were enclosed in scalding hot chambers for 30 days to purge their systems. This method was far more likely to bring about death from a heart attack or suffocation than it was to bring relief. Others believed that mercury treatments were the answer, but they caused scarcely less suffering.

Ehrlich and Compound Number 606

While some doctors were getting rich off unnecessary treatments for syphilis, others were devoting themselves to finding a cure for the disease. In 1905, Prussian scientist Fritz Schaudinn identified the cause of syphilis. It was a tiny corkscrew-shaped being that was not

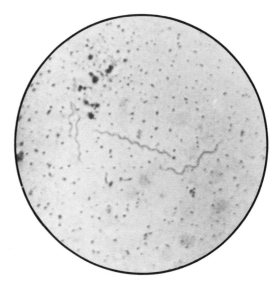

The syphilis protozoan is a tiny, corkscrew-shaped microorganism.

a bacterium, but another kind of microorganism called a **protozoan**.

In his search for a magic bullet, Paul Ehrlich chose the syphilis protozoan for target practice. The countless hours he had spent working with dyes to produce better slides led him to try these agents first. It was known that dyes attach themselves to parts of cells, so it was logical to ask if they could likewise become attached to a protozoan and kill it without harming anything else around it. Ehrlich was on the right track. In 1905, he proved that a dye known as trypan red was an able killer of the protozoan that caused African sleeping sickness. The red dye was the first artificially created cure for a specific infection.

Paul Ehrlich, the Father of Chemotherapy

that the compound did indeed work. An assistant had made a nearly disastrous mistake earlier in recording number 606 as a failure.

Ehrlich called compound number 606 Salvarsan and declared that he had found a magic bullet that would attack the syphilis protozoa. Always meticulous in his methods, Ehrlich performed exhaustive studies on Salvarsan before declaring it fit for human treatment in 1909. He later developed an improved version of the compound, called Neosalvarsan, which gave doctors an even safer tool in the fight against syphilis.

Few people have made as great an impact on their profession as Paul Ehrlich. From 1901 to 1913, his name was almost constantly in the running for a Nobel Prize. Although he won his only Nobel award—the 1908 Nobel Prize for physiology or medicine—for his work in immunology, the development of Salvarsan earned him the title of "Father of Chemotherapy."

Domagk's Desperate Test

Chemotherapy was such an effective weapon against the syphilis protozoan that scientists began to look for a magic bullet that would work against infectious diseases caused by bacteria. In the early 1900s, bacterial infections were still extremely dangerous, especially to young children. Strep throat could suddenly turn into scarlet fever, a serious illness that

Dyes, however, were not doing the trick with the syphilis protozoan, so Ehrlich switched to arsenic compounds. He screened more than 600 compounds to see if any was his magic bullet against syphilis, but one after another, they all failed to provide the results he wanted. It wasn't until a Japanese bacteriologist named Sahachiro Hata took a look at Ehrlich's research that a likely candidate was identified. Ehrlich had been puzzled by the failure of a compound labeled number 606 for which he had held high hopes. Hata's patient retesting showed had claimed thousands of lives in the mid-19th century, including five of the six children of the archbishop of Canterbury in a single month. Meningitis, a bacterial illness that had plagued both sides in the American Civil War, was on the rise again in the early 1900s. This disease usually struck children and was almost always fatal. But worst of all was pneumonia, which in 1901 was the most widespread and fatal of all diseases.

Until the 1930s, all searches for a magic bullet that would strike the agents responsible for bacterial infections ended in failure. Although scientists did know of a great number of materials that would destroy a bacteria colony in a test tube, many of those same substances had no effect on bacteria thriving in live, infected mice. Those that did kill the bacteria were so harmful to the surrounding tissues that they were useless.

Gerhard Domagk in his laboratory at I.G. Farbenindustrie in Germany

Into this void stepped yet **another German scientist**, Gerhard Domagk, who was born in eastern Germany in 1895. In 1927, Domagk's vast experience in medical research earned him a job as director of a spotless, modern research facility in Elberfeld, Germany. Domagk's laboratory was a subsidiary of a giant German corporation called I. G. Farbenindustrie, a company that was known for its expertise in making fabric dyes. As a part of Domagk's work in developing new drugs, he was expected to test some of the parent company's dyes to see if there were any marketable by-products. In 1932, Domagk began work on the company's newly patented red dye, Prontosil.

It didn't take Domagk long to discover that Prontosil was more than just a dye. Although the chemical seemed to be completely harmless to living tissue, it easily stopped the spread of hemolytic streptococcus bacteria, a scarlet fever-inducing microorganism. Laboratory mice infected with the bacteria recovered after receiving injections of the red dye. Further tests showed that Prontosil did not actually kill the bacteria, but it halted their growth by depriving them of vital nutrients.

No scientist could ever have had a more dramatic test of the value of his work than Domagk. In an age when even the smallest wounds could prove fatal, the importance of Domagk's experiments struck home when his own daughter suffered from an infected finger. Before long, the infection had spread and a dangerous fever was raging. There was no time to wait for exhaustive tests on the new drug; Domagk anxiously fed a small amount of the powdered dye to his daughter. Almost magically, the fever dropped and she recovered her health. I.G. Farbenindustrie quickly patented their new miracle cure, which was also able to perform its magic healing in cases of strep throat, tonsillitis, meningitis, gonorrhea, and pneumonia.

Further research destroyed the company's patent by proving that it wasn't the dye itself that produced results but rather a compound in the dye called sulfanilamide. Scientists went on to find other related compounds called **sulfa drugs**, which helped doctors combat many kinds of previously lethal infections. For this breakthrough, Domagk was voted the Nobel Prize for physiology or medicine in 1939.

Fleming's Ruined Experiment

While Domagk was being honored for his discovery of the healing capabilities of Prontosil, the discovery of the first **antibiotic**, one of the world's most important medical breakthroughs, was in danger of being buried in the forgotten files of dusty medical journals. As far back as the 1870s, scientists had been aware that some microorganisms manufacture substances that are harmful to other microorganisms. Although scientists saw the possibility of using these substances, which would one day be called antibiotics, to kill disease-causing microorganisms, they were unable to make it work.

Meanwhile, a young man named Alexander Fleming was growing up in Scotland. Fleming was not a dedicated student; in fact, he was reported to have chosen to attend St. Mary's Hospital Medical School because he was a good swimmer, and St. Mary's had an excellent swim team. Nevertheless, Fleming eventually became a private physician with a strong interest in research.

Fleming's research career was interrupted by the outbreak of World War I. While working in the medical corps, he was sickened by the primitive methods of treating war wounds. Some of the harsh remedies used to keep out the microorganisms that cause infection actually did more harm than good because they weakened the body's defenses. Anyone who submitted to the knife in an operating room was flirting with death, not so much from the wound itself as from infection and blood poisoning caused by the surgery. Even though a carbolic spray pioneered by the surgeon Joseph Lister had reduced problems of infection, it was far from a satisfactory solution to the problem.

Back in his laboratory after the war, Fleming toyed with ways to clear wounds of infectious microorganisms. As part of

*Alexander Fleming examines a **Penicillium** culture.*

that process, he grew cultures of a kind of staphylococcus bacteria that causes painful boils. One day in 1928, upon inspecting one of the containers on which the bacteria was growing, Fleming saw that it had been contaminated with fuzzy green mold colonies. A contaminated culture is of no use to a microbiologist, so Fleming was about to throw the ruined dish away when he noticed that the mold seemed to be limiting the growth of the bacteria. In fact, on closer

32

observation, he saw that it was *dissolving* the microorganisms.

Those tufted green colonies came from a genus of molds called *Penicillium*, from the Latin word for "little brush." Molds from this group can commonly be found on spoiled apples and oranges. While other scientists were searching so hard for a wonder drug that would combat bacteria, Fleming had stumbled upon one that had been sitting under their noses since the dawn of history.

Of course, Fleming could not just submit his contaminated dish as evidence of a new miracle drug. He had to perform a series of controlled experiments to prove his claim to the skeptical scientific world. After growing a pure strain of the *Penicillium*, Fleming filtered off fluid produced by the mold and added it to thriving cultures of staphylococcus bacteria. The killing agent in the fluid was so powerful that Fleming could actually see the bacteria disappear. Even when diluted to 1/100 of its original strength, it still destroyed bacteria colonies. Fleming found that the substance would kill a variety of harmful bacteria, not just staphylococcus. Further, his tests showed that it did not attack human tissue, and it caused no harmful side effects when given to mice and rabbits. Fleming called the fluid, which was the world's first antibiotic, **penicillin**.

Unfortunately, scientists did not leap to put Fleming's discovery to use. Extracting the pure antibiotic substance was a tricky task that required the skills of an expert chemist. Fleming was no chemist, and his attempts to purify penicillin usually left him with nothing but a headache and an inactive, syrupy glob. Whenever he was able to produce some active penicillin, local physicians didn't have a case to try it on, and when they did have a case, Fleming had no penicillin. With no way to make use of his discovery, Fleming watched as his penicillin experiments became just another batch of filler in the vast literature of the scientific journals.

Finding the Forgotten Files

It wasn't until 10 years later that Howard Florey and Ernst Chain, a pair of chemists at Oxford University in England, delved into the problem. They came across Fleming's paper on penicillin while hunting through books full of medical papers for clues about possible antibiotics. Between the two of them, Florey and Chain had the chemistry knowledge needed to produce active penicillin. The chemists found a way to separate the penicillin from the rest of the fluid produced by the mold. When the process was completed, a brown powder remained.

The powdered penicillin proved to be unbelievably powerful. When diluted to 1/2,000,000 of its original strength, it could still stop the growth of disease-causing bacteria. The pure penicillin was first

Howard Florey

Ernst Chain

tested in 1940 on eight mice infected with streptococcus bacteria, and the experiment was a success. Within 17 hours, the four mice that had not received penicillin were all dead, while the four that had been injected with the drug were still alive.

Every one of the many studies that were performed on penicillin indicated that the drug would be safe to try on a human. Florey and Chain, who had painstakingly collected a precious teaspoonful of the drug, were given a chance to test it when a police officer came down with an infection after he nicked himself shaving. The infection had spread until, four months later, he was almost certain to die. When the man was injected with penicillin, his condition immediately began to improve. Unfortunately, penicillin does not stay in the body for very long, so repeated doses are needed to effectively fight an infection. When the small supply of penicillin ran out, the infection flared up again, and the police officer died. The shortage of penicillin caused the second human case to end in failure as well. But the third attempt, using a 15-year-old boy who had contracted an infection during an operation, proved successful. Doctors were able to ration out just enough of the drug to pull him through.

The next step was to crank up production of penicillin on a huge scale. But this was 1941 and Great Britain had all that it could handle fighting a war with Nazi Germany, so the project had to be sent elsewhere.

The United States took up the challenge, and with the cooperation of scientists, industry, and government, enough penicillin was produced in 1943 to treat 500,000 people a month. Effective against more than 100 different kinds of bacteria, including those responsible for pneumonia, venereal disease, and blood poisoning, penicillin has been called the single most important discovery in the battle against disease. All three men, Fleming, Chain, and Florey, were included in the award of the Nobel Prize for physiology or medicine in 1945.

Thanks to Paul Ehrlich and the pioneers in chemotherapy who followed him, the diagnosis of a disease such as syphilis, strep throat, or pneumonia no longer has to be a death sentence. Today, chemotherapy is still an important weapon in the fight against disease, and scientists—possibly future Nobel Prize winners—continue to look for new and better magic bullets.

A technician manufactures penicillin in a laboratory in Toronto, Canada.

4

The Crippler

Most young people think that summer is the best time of the year. After spending all winter cooped up indoors with schoolwork, they look forward to three months of free time to spend with friends. It is a time of swimming, carnivals, movies, parades, ball games, and picnics. But what if all summer activities were cancelled? What if the pool, the beach, and any place where there were likely to be crowds of young people—that means *any* public place—were suddenly off-limits?

That's the way it was in parts of the United States during the first half of the 20th century. Parents did not restrict their children's activities to punish them; they did it out of the fear of an unseen killer that paralyzed its victims and could strike anyone at any time. The killer was a disease called poliomyelitis, better known

as polio. Children were especially susceptible to polio. In fact, the disease was sometimes referred to as infantile paralysis because people once thought that it struck only young children. For many years, the only way to protect children from this extremely contagious disease was to keep them away from anyone who might already be infected.

Before 1900, few people had even heard of polio, much less worried about it. Not that the disease was something new; throughout history, there have been many recorded examples of children becoming mysteriously paralyzed, which may have

This poster is a reminder that infantile paralysis, or polio, can strike the very young and leave them crippled for life.

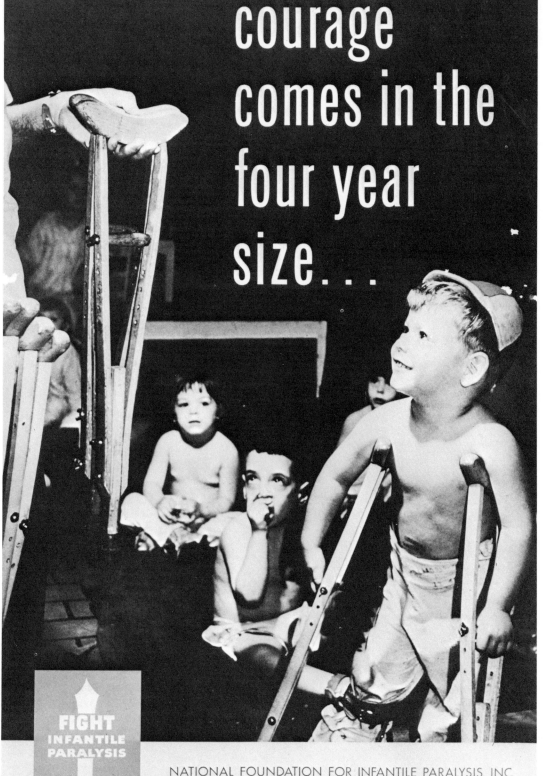

courage
comes in the
four year
size...

FIGHT
INFANTILE
PARALYSIS

NATIONAL FOUNDATION FOR INFANTILE PARALYSIS, INC.
INC. 120 Broadway, New York 5, N.Y.

Karl Landsteiner (front, third from left) won his Nobel Prize for discovering blood types, but he was also involved in polio research.

been the result of polio. But no one knew what caused the relatively rare cripplings, and they were accepted as just one of the dangers of childhood. By the 1900s, however, polio had become far more common and had spread not only to older children, but also to adults. When 750 cases popped up in New York City alone in 1907, the disease could no longer be ignored.

The Simplest Life-forms

Alarm spread in 1908 when Austrian-born scientist Karl Landsteiner, who was to win a Nobel Prize in 1930 for discovering blood types, confirmed people's suspicions that polio was contagious. Landsteiner had taken tissue from polio victims and squeezed its liquid through a special filter with openings small enough to trap bacteria. He had then injected the bacteria-free liquid into monkeys. When the monkeys came down with polio, Landsteiner could point to two conclusions. He had learned that polio is an infectious disease, which means it can be spread, and that the disease is caused by organisms that are even smaller than bacteria.

The tiny organism that is responsible

for polio is a mysterious bit of matter called a **virus**. The existence of viruses was discovered almost simultaneously in the 1890s by Russian Dmitri Ivanovski and by Martinus Beijerinck of Holland. Using the same methods that Landsteiner would later use in his polio experiments, both scientists strained fluid from a plant infected with tobacco mosaic disease through a filter fine enough to trap bacteria. They found that even without the bacteria, the fluid still contained something that would infect plants with the disease. Beijerinck called the disease-causing substance a virus, which means "poison" in Latin.

Although they have now been photographed with electron microscopes, little is known about viruses to this day. They are the simplest life-forms that have been discovered, and the smallest as well. The largest virus is about .3 micron, which is only 1/10 the size of the average bacterium, and the smallest is about .01 micron. (One micron is equal to .001 millimeters.) Viruses, which can be rod-shaped or spherical, don't seem to act like any other substance, living or nonliving. Doctors do know, however, that they are responsible for many diseases; in fact, when you come down with an illness that cannot be diagnosed, your doctor will probably guess that it is some sort of virus. The list of illnesses caused by viruses includes influenza, measles, colds, and, as Landsteiner discovered, polio.

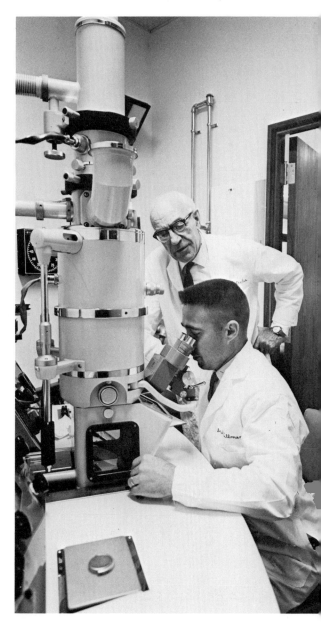

Most viruses can only be seen through an electron microscope.

Polio victim Franklin Delano Roosevelt was active in the fight against the disease.

In Polio's Shadow

The poliomyelitis virus is a sphere-shaped microorganism so tiny that 25 million of them can fit on the head of a pin. Like most other viruses, the polio virus was a mystery to scientists in the early 20th century, except for the fact that it was known to attack the central nervous system. The word *poliomyelitis* comes from two Greek words meaning "gray marrow," indicating that it is a disease that thrives inside the gray matter of the brain and the spinal cord. Mild forms of polio result in flulike symptoms such as fever, headache, sore throat, and vomiting, which last only about 24 hours. More severe cases have the same symptoms as mild forms, but last longer and can result in nerve damage. Damaged nerves are unable to trigger responses in muscles, which wither away, leaving victims with varying degrees of paralysis. When muscles used for breathing are paralyzed, the victim can die of suffocation.

As the years went by, the polio epidemic continued to get worse. In 1911, nearly 4,000 Swedes were stricken with the disease. Five years later, 27,000 new cases of polio were reported in the United States, 6,000 of them ending in death. The experience of its most famous victim illustrates how suddenly and quietly polio can do its damage. In 1921, 39-year-old Franklin Delano Roosevelt went to bed early one evening complaining of chills. That minor problem soon escalated into

John Enders

fever and pain in his joints. Roosevelt recovered from the chills and fever within a week, but he would never get over the damage that polio had done to his legs. Roosevelt, who went on to become the only four-term president in United States history, was never again able to walk without assistance.

While the shadow cast by polio continued to spread over the world, medical researchers were getting nowhere with the disease. The polio virus was very difficult to work with. Scientists, who needed a large enough sample of the virus to make a vaccine, had only been able to grow the virus in nerve tissue, preferably the spinal cords of monkeys. The use of monkeys for mass experiments was enormously expensive. In addition, viruses grown in nerve tissue are especially dangerous because they are very powerful and if made into a vaccine, threaten humans with dangerous side effects. The only solution seemed to be to find another way to grow the polio virus.

Learning from the Mumps

The problems posed by the polio virus were solved by a research team led by a Connecticut-born virologist named John Enders. During World War II, Enders was involved in preparing a short-term vaccine for the mumps, which, like polio, is caused by a virus. He then teamed up with Thomas Weller of Michigan and Frederick Robbins of Alabama to study viruses. Enders's research team did not immediately examine the lethal viruses like the one responsible for polio, but rather they began with nuisance ones that caused relatively mild, although bothersome, illnesses such as the mumps. In the course of their studies, the three men developed improved methods of culturing viruses.

After completing some experiments with the mumps virus, the Enders team still had a few leftover culture flasks of human skin and muscle tissue. Instead of throwing them out, they decided to see if they could grow the polio virus in the cultures. Not only were they successful, but they were able to break through the barrier that had kept polio research at a standstill for decades. The Enders team showed that the polio virus could be grown on tissue other than nerve tissue, which meant that there was a good chance that a safe vaccine could be made.

The three men also came up with a technique whereby a researcher could tell whether or not the harmful virus was growing in a test animal without infecting another animal. All that was needed was a dye to detect acid produced by growing tissue. If the virus was thriving, it damaged the tissue culture and made it unable to produce the color-changing acid. If the virus was not growing, the healthy cells

Frederick Robbins

Thomas Weller

During the 1950s, large metal tanks called respirators or iron lungs saved the lives of many people whose chest muscles had been paralyzed by polio, leaving them unable to breathe for themselves.

would produce the acid, and the tissue would change color.

These advances paved the way for other scientists to come up with safe and effective polio vaccines. Less than six months after Enders, Weller, and Robbins were awarded the 1954 Nobel Prize for their work with the polio virus, the first polio vaccine was pronounced a success. The continual polio epidemics that had swept through the United States, peaking in 1955 with 58,000 new cases of the disease, was brought to an abrupt halt with vaccines developed by Jonas Salk in 1954 and Albert Sabin in 1961. By 1963, polio claimed only 400 new victims in the entire year, and 10 years later, the once-raging disease had become a medical oddity. Although many researchers had a hand in the triumph over polio, it was the Nobel Prize-winning team of Enders, Weller, and Robbins that bridged the gap to lead the way to a successful conclusion.

44

5

The Killer Mosquitoes

One of the longest-running feuds of all time has been that between humans and mosquitoes. Mosquitoes have driven more than one gentle person into a murderous fury by ruining a nature hike or a beautiful summer evening with their annoying little jabs. But these insects can cause far more damage than just a mosquito bite. Over the centuries, they have secretly carried on a form of germ warfare that has caused the deaths of millions of people. It was not until the 1800s that scientists were able to pin these deaths on the activities of this common insect and begin to map a strategy to fight back.

Walter Reed infects volunteers with yellow fever so that he can study the course of the disease.

Marsh Fever

The mosquito has made malaria the most widespread infectious disease in the world. Unlike the violent plagues that have swept through entire countries, killing hundreds of people within a few days, malaria works in a subtle way. It introduces itself with chills and a high fever, which may mysteriously disappear only to return at regular intervals. Victims also suffer from headaches, nausea, and muscle aches as the disease slowly weakens them to the point of exhaustion. Those whom malaria doesn't kill outright are often left with no resistance to ward off other illnesses.

During the past 2,000 years, many cultures came close to discovering how malaria is spread, but the final connection

45

to the mosquito was not made until the end of the 19th century. The disease was blamed instead on the prime breeding ground of the mosquito, the swamp. The forerunners of the Romans, the Etruscans, understood as early as the third century B.C. that the incidence of malaria could be reduced by draining marshy areas, and for hundreds of years after that, the disease was commonly referred to as marsh fever. Even its modern name, malaria, which comes from two Greek words meaning "bad air," reflects the belief that the disease is caused by poisonous swamp gases.

Like most diseases, malaria has caused a few turns in the course of history. Many military and exploratory expeditions throughout the centuries have been affected by the disease. Some historians theorize that the fall of the Roman Empire was aided by a general weakness of the population due to widespread malaria. They also speculate that the Germanic tribes that conquered Rome were eventually forced to abandon the city because they couldn't cope with the malaria problem. Hundreds of years later, the American Civil War might have ended sooner had Union troops not been forced to postpone their attack on the key fortress of Vicksburg because of a malaria epidemic. The disease was still a problem less than a century ago when it helped to

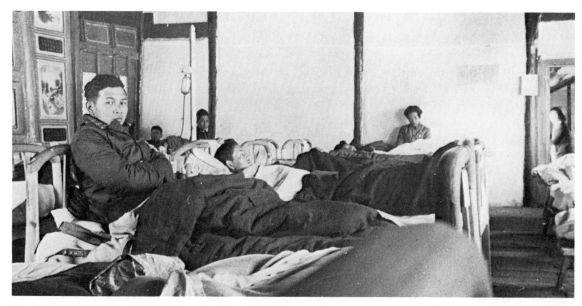

During World War II, this hospital on the Burma Road was intended for those wounded in combat, but it quickly filled up with malaria victims instead.

Charles Laveran

thwart work on the Panama Canal for many years.

Laveran Finds a Puzzle Piece

The cause of marsh fever was a two-part puzzle that was solved by a pair of military surgeons from different countries. The first half of the puzzle was assembled by a French doctor named Charles Laveran. After serving with the French army in the Franco-Prussian War, Laveran was stationed at a military hospital in Algeria, where he was kept busy treating a steady stream of malaria patients.

Although Laveran was unable to keep many of these patients alive, he took advantage of his situation by studying the disease.

Like other scientists before him, Laveran noticed that there was a black pigment in the blood of malaria victims that changed their spleens from red to dark brown. Focusing his microscope on a drop of the dark-colored blood, Laveran discovered a host of crescent-shaped microorganisms equipped with tiny whiplike "tails" that helped them to move. When he saw the tails, or **flagella**, the doctor knew that these microorganisms were not bacteria, which had proven to be the culprit in most of the recent studies of disease, but were protozoa. The black pigment found in the blood of malaria victims turned out to be waste material from this microorganism. This particular protozoan was a parasite that lived off the red blood cells of its host; and the discovery that it causes malaria earned a Nobel Prize for Laveran in 1907.

Ross Completes the Puzzle

The second half of the malaria puzzle, how the parasite gets into a red blood cell in the first place, was put together by Ronald Ross. Ross, whose father was a British general, was born in 1857 while his family was stationed in India. He took a roundabout route in getting to his Nobel research; in his younger days, he seemed to study everything but medicine. After trying his hand at poetry, writing, mathematics, mechanics, languages, and philosophy, however, Ross finally earned a degree in medicine in England and then returned to his native India in 1881.

In the wet, steamy Indian jungles, Ross became obsessed with the study of the insect that was making life miserable for both the natives and the British troops, the mosquito. He soon came to the conclusion that the mosquito, Laveran's protozoa, and the dreaded swamp fever were all tied together somehow, and he set about trying to prove that connection.

Rarely, if ever, has a scientific researcher plodded on in the face of obstacles as mountainous as those that confronted Ross in his studies. Except for the advice of British surgeon Patrick Manson, Ross was completely on his own, and any money used on his experiments had to come out of his own pocket. One of his investments was a portable microscope that he invented to take with him into the jungle, usually his only research facility.

Wherever Ross turned for help, he was met with incompetence, indifference, and superstition. Most people still believed that marsh air or night air caused malaria and that his experiments were a waste of time. Even when the scientist did manage to put an experiment together, it often had to be scrapped when his supply of mosquitoes suddenly died out or refused

Ronald Ross

to bite, or when the patients he had recruited grew tired of being bitten and deserted him. There were times when Ross would finally get a satisfactory laboratory set up only to have the army transfer him to a station in a different part of India. He often had to handle his staggering work load while reeling from the effects of the very disease he was studying.

Despite the odds, Ross continued to search for a link between the mosquito

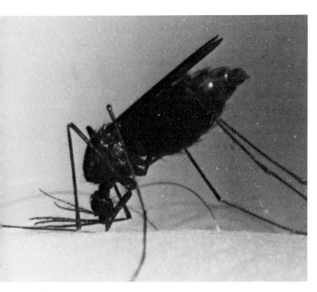

An Anopheles *mosquito prepares to bite.*

and the malaria protozoan. Over the years, he captured, raised, and dissected thousands of mosquitoes but was unable to prove his theory. What he didn't know was that of all the different kinds of mosquitoes in the area, the only species that carried malaria was the *Anopheles* mosquito. Further, of the over 400 kinds of *Anopheles* mosquitoes, only 60 have turned out to be malaria carriers.

On August 20, 1897, another of the doctor's experiments was coming to a frustrating end. He was trying to study the *Anopheles* mosquito, but the usual problems with keeping mosquitoes alive had taken their toll, and he had only one insect left. Ross allowed the mosquito to feast on a malaria patient, and then he laboriously picked apart all the insect's

organs, as he had with countless other mosquitoes. Finding nothing out of the ordinary, Ross had nearly given up when he came at last to the insect's stomach. There he found what he had been searching for all this time. The insect's stomach contained the black pigment granules that indicated the presence of Laveran's parasite.

Ross completed his proof of the connection between malaria and the mosquito in 1898 by using the protozoa found in the mosquitoes to infect birds with malaria. His work established that it was the bite of the female *Anopheles* mosquito that introduced the protozoa into the bloodstream. These organisms then attacked and destroyed blood cells, causing chills, fever, and sometimes death. An uninfected mosquito turned into a carrier by sucking the blood of a malaria victim. Because of a quirk of the Nobel voting system, Ronald Ross was awarded the Nobel Prize for physiology or medicine in 1902, five years before it was awarded to Laveran.

In spite of the work of the malaria pioneers, the disease continued to rage out of control for decades. By the 1930s, malaria was spreading at an alarming rate, with an estimated 100 million new cases and 3 million malaria deaths in the world in a single year. Because protozoa could not be cultured in test tubes as bacteria could, scientists did not know how to study the disease. Little progress was made until a solution was offered by another Nobel Prize winner, discussed in the next chapter, who wasn't even a doctor.

Yellow Fever Rampage

While some scientists were studying malaria, others were concentrating on another equally mysterious disease, which occurred in some of the same geographic areas as the dangerous marsh fever. This disease was so widespread and had been feared for so long that it was known by more than 150 names, including yellow jack and its most common name, yellow fever. These names referred to the fact that a victim's skin and the whites of a victim's eyes were turned yellow by the illness. Intense pain and weakness accompanied the fever, and victims sometimes vomited black blood shortly before dying.

If it weren't for yellow fever, the United States might not have reached the size it is today. At the beginning of the 19th century, France owned a vast section of North American territory that stretched from New Orleans to Montana. In 1802, the French emperor Napoleon I sent an army expedition to the New World to quiet a rebellion in the Caribbean and to take stock of his holdings in North America. The soldiers had barely landed in the Caribbean islands, however, when they were devastated by a savage wave of yellow fever. Of the 33,000 men sent to the New World, only 4,000 escaped the epidemic. Historians speculate that this so soured Napoleon on the disease-ridden New World that he wanted nothing more to do with it. One year later, the United States was surprised with an offer from Napoleon to sell France's North American lands at a very low price, an offer that was quickly accepted in a transaction called the Louisiana Purchase.

Yellow fever occasionally swept up into the more northernly climates. In 1793, the city of Philadelphia was ravaged by an outbreak that killed a 10th of the population. But more often, the disease flourished in warm, wet areas of the world. New Orleans, a perfect candidate for a yellow fever epidemic, was brought to a standstill in 1853 when one-fourth of the population was infected with the disease, about a third of whom died.

After more than 200 soldiers died of yellow fever while stationed in Havana, Cuba, during the Spanish-American War, the United States decided to take action. They appointed a commission led by army doctor Major Walter Reed to study the disease. Not long after the mosquito was identified as an accomplice in the spreading of malaria, Reed's group discovered that the insect was also responsible for yellow fever. They found that it was specifically the bite of the female *Aedes aegypti* mosquito that spread the disease. These mosquitoes were not the noisy insects that most people were familiar with. They could

This illustration, which appeared in Harpers Weekly *in 1879, shows a group of people fleeing to Kansas to get away from yellow fever.*

suck infected blood and carry it to another person without being noticed.

Reed's discoveries, while valuable, did not automatically make the world safe from yellow fever. Although the disease could be controlled in the United States by destroying the swamp breeding grounds of the *Aedes aegypti*, this did not offer protection in the tropics, where it was not possible to completely wipe out this kind of habitat. The tropics remained as dangerous as ever.

Taming the Deadly Virus

While scientists did not know how to attack the protozoa responsible for malaria, they were more optimistic about finding a cure for yellow fever. Studies showed that in regions where yellow fever had existed for hundreds of years, such as in Africa, native populations seemed to be virtually immune to the disease. It was left to Max Theiler to come up with a vaccine that would induce this same immunity in those whom nature hadn't protected.

Max Theiler was a South African, born in 1899, who spent most of his life in the United States. Although he did not have the advanced education of most researchers, Theiler was an expert on tropical diseases when he was only in his twenties, and he put his knowledge to work by tackling the dangerous subject of yellow fever. It was not an area of research that attracted the timid; while Theiler was delving into the problem, eight yellow fever researchers died of the disease they were investigating.

Just prior to Theiler's research, the question of whether yellow fever was caused by a virus or a bacterium had finally been established. It was definitely a virus, one of those mysterious microorganisms so tiny that they could not be seen with the most powerful microscopes available at the time. That was bad news for scientists, since viruses were so much more difficult to work with than bacteria. They only grew in living tissue, and it appeared that monkeys were the only animals that could be used in experiments with viruses that affected humans. This made research impractical, since no laboratory could afford the thousands of

Max Theiler

monkeys it would require for thorough research.

Like other scientists had done in the past, Theiler tried to infect mice, which are much cheaper than monkeys, with yellow fever. He was unsuccessful until he thought of going right into the mouse brain. Theiler injected a solution containing fine bits of infected monkey liver into the heads of mice, and the animals quickly developed yellow fever and died.

As Theiler continued to pass yellow fever from one mouse to another, a change took place in the virus. Although it was still deadly to mice, it began to lose its power to kill monkeys. The first monkey Theiler injected with the virus from a mouse died of yellow fever almost immediately. After the virus had been passed through several more mice, another monkey was injected. Although it contracted yellow fever, this monkey managed to survive. The virus was passed through more mice, and a third monkey was then injected. This monkey showed no signs of yellow fever. It seemed that Theiler had succeeded in "taming" the deadly yellow fever virus.

By taming the yellow fever virus, Theiler opened up the possibility that humans could be vaccinated with the weakened virus and build up an immunity to yellow fever. He continued to weaken the virus by passing it from mouse to mouse. A spot check on his 176th passage told him that a change had occurred; now the virus did not even harm mice. This good news, however, did not mean that the virus was ready to be used as a vaccine for humans. Even in this mild form, the virus would attack the nervous system. Building on the work that Theiler had pioneered, research teams developed a new strain of virus that didn't affect the nervous system, paving the way for a safe vaccine.

The results of Theiler's work are perhaps best illustrated in some statistics from World War II. Although United States servicemen were operating in areas where the *Aedes aegypti* mosquito still thrived, not one soldier died of yellow fever during the war, thanks to the vaccine. The danger of yellow fever still lurks in tropical areas today, and some African nations require all visitors to be vaccinated. Max Theiler can be thanked for making such vaccination possible, and the Nobel committee did just that in awarding him the 1951 Nobel Prize for physiology or medicine.

Although humans were the victors in the fight against the *Aedes aegypti* mosquito, other insect-related diseases—such as malaria—continue to take lives. But people like Charles Laveran, Ronald Ross, and Max Theiler laid the groundwork for the discovery of new weapons to use against disease.

6

The Disease of Soldiers

Had the land-hungry French emperor, Napoleon I, been as brilliant at medical research as he was at battle strategy, French might well be the dominant language in the world today. Unfortunately for Napoleon and hundreds of thousands of soldiers, the most thorough preparations, the most powerful weapons, and the best-trained armies in the world were no match for some of the smallest insects. The damage done to Napoleon's troops in the New World by the yellow fever mosquito was nothing compared to the catastrophe brought on by another tiny enemy during what was supposed to be

This machine was used to delouse soldiers to stop the spread of yellow fever.

the French emperor's greatest triumph.

In 1812, after adding most of Europe to his empire, Napoleon assembled a magnificent army of 600,000 men and set out to conquer Russia. A few months later, Napoleon's army straggled back to France reduced by over 500,000 men. Legend has it that the bold French ambitions failed because the soldiers could not cope with the bitter Russian winter. The evidence shows, however, that most of the French casualties were not caused by Russian bullets or cold weather, but by a disease called typhus.

Typhus has been called "the soldier's enemy" because it has burrowed its way into military camps during most of the famous wars in history. With more than 8,000 of his troops sidelined by typhus during the American Revolution, American general Nathanael Greene suffered defeats that healthy troops could have turned into victories. The suffering caused by typhus during the Crimean War, which lasted from 1853 to 1856, was ghastly, as the disease claimed nearly one million lives. During the early months of World War I, 150,000 Serbians died of typhus, a tragedy that, ironically, scared away potential invaders. Serbia's battle with typhus pales, however, when compared to the epidemic suffered by the Russians at the end of that same war. Nearly seven million Russians are believed to have developed typhus within five years after World War I, with about three million of those cases ending in death.

Typhus is characterized by a high fever, muscle aches, headaches, a weak pulse, a red rash that can turn brown, delirium, and coma. Even when little else had been learned about it, typhus was known to be a disease of dirt. Whenever people were thrown together in crowded, unsanitary conditions, such as those associated with wartime, severe typhus epidemics were likely to break out. As a result, army camps and squalid areas where the very poor lived almost on top of each other were always likely targets for an attack.

Nicolle and the Body Louse

The person who pinned down the cause of the deadly typhus epidemics was Charles Nicolle, a Frenchman whose discoveries came a century too late to save Napoleon. Born in 1866, Nicolle followed his father and brother into medicine in spite of the fact that he was deaf. After studying microbiology at the Pasteur Institute, Nicolle became interested in investigating typhus.

It seemed strange to Nicolle that a disease that was usually associated with filth seemed to thrive in hospitals, of all places. But while he was visiting a hospital in Tunisia, he had two sudden realizations. He noticed that when there was an outbreak of typhus at a hospital, it rarely spread beyond the hospital doors and that doctors and nurses often caught the disease. Typhus, in fact, had a solid reputation as a killer of doctors. Nicolle reasoned that since a patient's clothing was taken away upon entrance to a hospital, there must be something on the body that spread the disease. Evidence pointed to body lice, tiny bloodsucking insects that attached themselves to humans and animals. It had been established that close contact was needed to spread typhus, which coincided with the fact that lice could crawl but were unable to fly.

Nicolle used monkeys to prove the connection between lice and typhus. He was able to give the disease to healthy animals by transferring lice to them from infected animals. Later studies showed that typhus is not caused by the louse itself, but by a parasite of the louse that

Body lice are equipped with hooked feet to hold on to human body hair and beak-like mouths that can pierce skin.

attacks the human body. This viruslike organism, called rickettsia prowazeki, was named for Howard Ricketts and Stanislas von Prowazek, two men who died of typhus while researching the disease.

Lifesaving Poison

The problem with typhus, as with malaria, was what to do about it once scientists knew what caused the disease. Vaccines for typhus were attempted but proved ineffective. Delousing suspected carriers could help control epidemics once they had started, but that was far from an ideal solution. What was needed was a wide-scale method of destroying the body louse.

The obvious solution was to come up with an effective **insecticide**, or poison, that would kill the typhus louse; but scientists were unsuccessful until Paul Müller set out to solve the problem. Müller, who was a brilliant chemist, was hired by the Swiss corporation J. R. Geigy in 1925 to develop new dyes. In 1935, he was assigned to the new task of discovering a chemical that would destroy insects. The company was particularly interested in developing a mothproofing product. Müller's laboratory was soon swarming with so many flies and plant lice that his colleagues began to make fun of him. But Müller doggedly pursued his goal and gradually settled on one compound that killed insects of many kinds with unusual effectiveness. This substance was called dichlorodiphenyl-trichloroethane, or DDT for short. First synthesized by a German pharmacist in 1873, it was made from fairly common components: chlorine, alcohol, and sulfuric acid.

DDT seemed to be the chemical Müller had been looking for. It was different from other insecticides in that it was not a

Paul Müller

quick killer. An insect that came in contact with the poison showed no effects at all for about 20 minutes and might not die for hours. Although it acted slowly, DDT's advantage was that it retained its killing power for a long time. While most insecticides lasted only a few hours, DDT could go on killing for days. Müller's chemical was also lightweight, inexpensive, and deadly to many different kinds of insects, including the body louse. In 1944, after it was determined that the new insecticide did not affect people or animals, DDT was ready to be used against typhus.

The United States Army tested the chemical during the latter days of World War II. Shortly after the city of Naples, Italy, was captured by Allied troops, a typhus epidemic broke out. Given the past history of the disease and the masses of homeless people and war refugees milling about, it was a very dangerous situation. A United States general ordered the entire city sprayed with DDT, and as a result, the epidemic was controlled. After centuries of preying on army camps, an epidemic of the disease of soldiers was stopped cold.

Conditions were almost perfect for the spread of a massive typhus outbreak at the end of the war. Prisoners who had escaped or had been freed from horrid, unsanitary concentration camps were like thousands of lit fuses spreading through Europe, ready to set off another wave of death. This time, however, refugees entering a new country were routinely dusted with DDT, and the horrible typhus plagues like those that had followed World War I were avoided.

DDT was also an effective killer of the *Anopheles* mosquito, which meant that there was finally a weapon to use against malaria. Armed with the powerful insecticide, pilots could spray remote jungles and swamps to wipe out breeding mosquitoes. For the first time, real progress was made in limiting damage

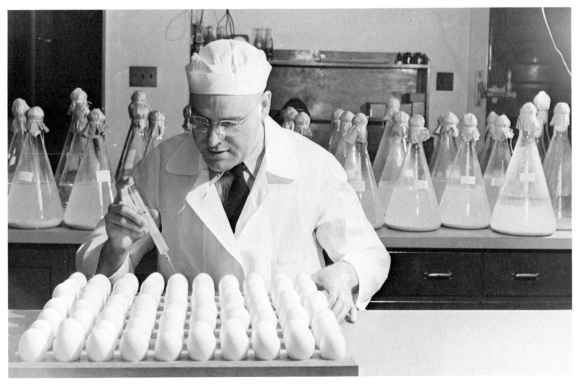

During the 1940s, Dr. Herrald R. Cox developed a method of making typhus vaccine from infected eggs.

from malaria. While there were over one million cases of malaria in the United States in 1940, eight years later that number had fallen to 10,000. Greece lost 1,856 citizens to malaria in 1942. With improved mosquito control, the death toll plunged to 14 in 1950.

Although initially received with great enthusiasm, DDT has turned out to be a mixed blessing. By the 1960s, people had begun to realize that DDT wasn't as harmless as it had first appeared to be.

Not only were its long-lasting effects demonstrated to be extremely dangerous to humans as well as to animals, but strains of mosquitoes have developed that can survive DDT encounters. Although it is still being used in some parts of the world, nearly all uses of DDT were banned in the United States in 1972. Nonetheless, Paul Müller's work probably saved the lives of millions of people, and for that he was awarded the Nobel Prize for physiology or medicine in 1948.

60

7

Persian Fire

Unlike many other diseases, diabetes mellitus, usually called diabetes, is as much a part of the present as it was of the past. There are more diabetics in the world today than there have ever been before, thanks to the efforts of Frederick Banting. This does not mean that Banting was a failure as a doctor. Success in the fight against diabetes is best measured by the increase rather than the decrease of the number of diabetics simply because not long ago people who had the disease didn't live very long. While there is not yet a cure for diabetes, Banting's work with **insulin** has allowed diabetics to

Charles Best (left) and Frederick Banting (right) work together to find a way to treat diabetes.

control their disease so that they can live long, active lives.

Diabetes was one of the earliest diseases to be documented in history, probably because its symptoms are so striking. There are records of a disease called honey urine, which plagued people more than 3,500 years ago. Because one of its symptoms was unusually sweet urine like that caused by diabetes, researchers believe that honey urine was actually diabetes. In the ancient Middle East, diabetes was called Persian fire because of the the constant maddening thirst that accompanied the disease. Other symptoms include hunger, weight loss, and excessive urination.

Before diabetes could be controlled, doctors had to stand by and watch helplessly while the disease took its terrible toll on its victims and eventually killed them. If left unchecked, diabetes can cause blindness, kidney failure, and heart disease, and can damage limbs so badly that they must be amputated. Its victims appear to be starving to death, even though they may be eating much more than a nondiabetic person. In the 19th century, doctors found that a strict diet low in carbohydrates could prolong the life of a diabetic, but the diets were nearly impossible to follow and the patients usually died before long.

Mystery Cells

By the early 20th century, doctors had learned that diabetes is the inability of the body to **metabolize** sugar, or turn it into energy and building blocks for the cells. This dysfunction is more serious than it sounds. Although food is made up of proteins, fats, and carbohydrates, the body gets most of its energy from carbohydrates. When carbohydrates enter the body, they are broken down into a simple sugar called glucose. In a person that does not have diabetes, the glucose is converted into energy, but a diabetic is unable to complete this process and the glucose builds up in the bloodstream and the urine. Some important clues to the mystery of why diabetics can't metabolize sugar were found in research done in the late 1800s.

In 1889, two German scientists, Oskar Minkowski and Joseph von Mering, were studying digestive enzymes when they discovered that by removing the pancreas from a dog they could make the animal diabetic. The obvious solution that diabetes must be caused by the lack of the digestive enzymes produced by the pancreas was proven to be wrong when scientists found that simply stopping the flow of enzymes did not cause the disease. It appeared that the pancreas must secrete some other substance needed by the body to metabolize sugar.

Once a connection had been found between the pancreas and diabetes, scientists became interested in a discovery that had been announced by medical student Paul Langerhans in 1869. Langerhans had discovered that the pancreas contained certain cells that did not secrete digestive enzymes, although he had no idea what they *did* do. Scientists speculated that these cells, which were called islets of Langerhans, produced something that allowed the body to metabolize sugar. Repeated attempts to isolate this substance, however, were unsuccessful, and most scientists gave up the search.

Childhood Memories

That's the way things stood when Frederick Banting was growing up in Ontario, Canada, where he had been born in 1891. There is a popular story that when

62

Frederick Banting

Banting was a young boy, one of his best friends suddenly became so ill she could no longer play with him. Her body wasted away, and she died a short time later. Banting was told that his friend had diabetes and that there was nothing medical science could do about the disease. It is said that the pain of that loss was repeated later when another of his friends died of the same illness.

Whether or not this tale is true, no one could have suspected that young Banting would one day find the key to treating diabetes.

Although Banting's father had hoped his son would become a minister, Banting decided to study medicine in college. Putting his medical training to use in World War I, Banting suffered a wound so serious that doctors were determined to amputate his arm. He refused to allow the amputation, however, and supervised his own treatment until he was fully recovered. Without that arm, he might not have been able to perform later crucial experiments.

After the war, Banting set up a medical practice in Ontario and quickly found out that medicine was not an automatic road to fortune. Completely frustrated in his attempts to attract patients, Banting only earned about $12 during his first three months on the job. He realized that he could not survive at that rate, so he accepted a job teaching physiology at the University of Western Ontario.

In 1920, while he was preparing some material on the pancreas for his class, Banting found that he didn't know enough about the subject to give a good lecture. A conscientious teacher, Banting turned to medical journals to do further research on the organ. He took special notice of an article that discussed the connection between secretions produced by the islets of Langerhans and diabetes. It suddenly occurred to Banting that if he were to tie

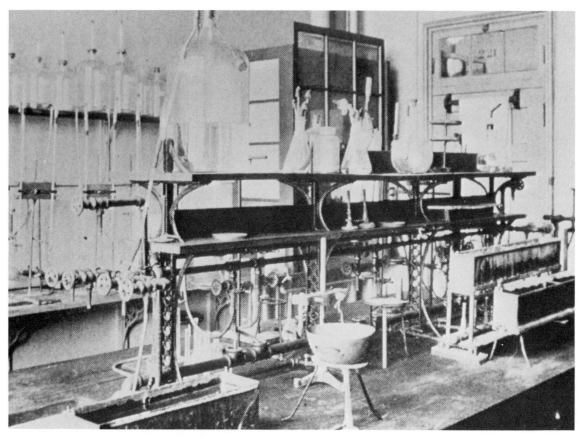

Banting and Best discovered insulin in this lab at the University of Toronto.

off the ducts of a living pancreas, where the islets of Langerhans are located, he might be able to collect some of the secretions and see what they were.

Insulin

In order to follow through on his ideas, Banting needed to find a laboratory and some test animals. Since there were no facilities available at the University of Western Ontario, Banting's supervisor suggested that he contact John J. R. Macleod at the University of Toronto. At first Macleod did not want to have anything to do with Banting's experiments, but he finally relented and gave Banting the use of his laboratory and a few dogs while he was in Scotland for the summer.

In spite of his help, Macleod made it clear that he didn't think Banting's idea would work.

After recruiting a biochemistry student named Charles Best, who had experience measuring blood sugar, to help him with his experiments, Banting was ready to get started. The two men tied off the pancreatic ducts of several dogs and then settled down for a nerve-wracking six-to-eight-week waiting period. After six weeks, they opened the animals back up and to their dismay found that the ducts had broken open. They quickly repeated the experiment on a new set of dogs, this time using a different kind of thread to tie off the ducts. Their time was running out, so after only four weeks, they checked the dogs and found that the new thread had held.

Banting and Best removed the pancreases from two of the dogs, ground the organs up, and extracted a small amount of fluid. The two men then used the fluid to treat a dog that was in a deep coma, very near death from diabetes. After an injection of just a few drops, the dog began to perk up, and the level of sugar in its blood dropped. With further injections, the dog was quickly brought back to relatively good health.

The substance produced by the islets of Langerhans, which was eventually called insulin, turned out to be the essential ingredient in metabolizing sugar. Banting realized that a diabetic would need several injections of insulin

Best (left) and Banting (right) pose with Marjorie, the first diabetic dog to be brought out of a coma with insulin.

every day, which meant that a substantial source of the substance was needed. He also knew that before injections of insulin could be used for humans, he must ensure that it was safe.

65

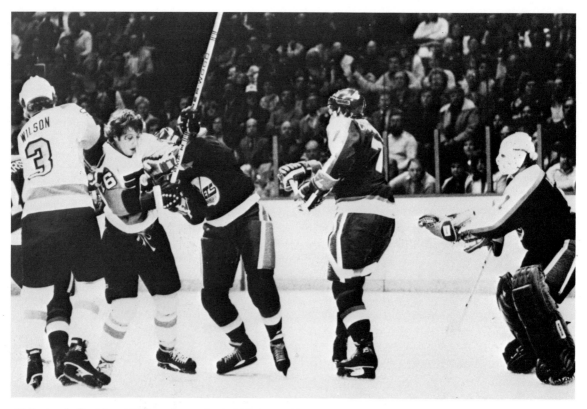

Although Bobby Clarke (number 16) is a diabetic, the disease did not stop him from having a long, successful career in professional hockey.

Banting turned to butchered cows for increased quantities of insulin and to James Collip for help with purifying and standardizing the doses of the substance. By January of 1922, they were ready to try insulin on a human being.

Banting's first patient was Leonard Thompson, a young boy who had battled diabetes for two years with the usual treatment of a strict diet and fasting. Thompson had wasted away to 65 pounds

and was near death when doctors started him on a program of insulin injections. Thompson's health began to improve immediately, and he was soon able to leave the hospital. The medical world hailed the miraculous news that an effective means of controlling another tragic disease had been found.

Eventually, methods of synthetically manufacturing many different kinds of insulin were developed, and scientists no longer had to rely entirely on animals. Although the disease can be controlled, diabetes is still a dangerous and widespread illness. There are about 11 million diabetics in the United States alone, where the disease is responsible for nearly 150,000 deaths every year. With careful attention to a prescribed medical program, however, diabetics can take part in the most strenuous of physical occupations, including professional sports.

Banting shared the 1923 Nobel Prize for physiology or medicine not with Charles Best, as might be expected, but with John J. R. Macleod. Distressed by the oversight, Banting showed his appreciation for Best's work by acknowledging his contribution to the discovery of insulin and giving him half of the prize money.

John J. R. Macleod

Charles Best

8

The Missing Ingredient

It has taken humans thousands of years at a cost of untold numbers of lives to understand that disease can come about not only because of what's there, but also because of what's missing. Until fairly recently, doctors blamed most illnesses on body invaders such as viruses or bacteria. By the late 19th century, however, researchers had begun to suspect that some foods contain certain substances that people need to stay healthy. When these substances, called vitamins, are missing from a person's diet, he or she falls victim to such deadly diseases as scurvy and beriberi.

Before the discovery of vitamins, people unknowingly protected themselves from the diseases caused by vitamin deficiency simply by eating a wide variety of foods. There were some people, however, such as explorers and sailors, who were often cut off from their usual range of food choices for long periods of time. Members of this group ran a high risk of becoming mysteriously ill and even dying.

In 1498, the Portuguese explorer Vasco da Gama successfully completed a voyage around the southern tip of Africa to Asia. The trip was far from successful, however, for 100 of the 160 crew members, who suffered bleeding gums and fever and finally became so pitifully weak that they died before reaching their destination. The disease from which they suffered

Modern technology enables a chemist to test a dehydrated vegetable sample for vitamin B. Not long ago, people weren't even aware that vitamins existed.

For hundreds of years, sailors on long voyages were in danger of dying from mysterious diseases like scurvy and beriberi.

was known as scurvy, and it attacked the British navy for centuries.

Meanwhile, the Japanese navy was experiencing equally dreadful attacks of a disease called beriberi. The name of the illness means "I cannot," which described the hidious fate of its victims, who became too weak and sick to do anything and often ended up paralyzed. Even those who survived were left in such a ravaged condition that they could no longer work. This same illness spread on land to the Dutch colonies in the East Indies in the late 19th century. It was said that a three-month jail sentence in Java or Sumatra was the same as the death penalty, such was the strength of the beriberi epidemic in the island prisons.

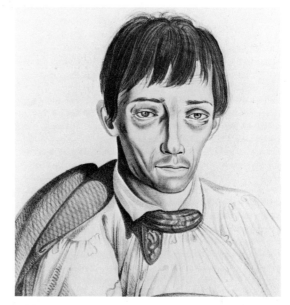

This drawing from 1842 of a man suffering from scurvy illustrates the debilitating effect the disease has on its victims.

70

Disregarded Evidence

Had the medical profession taken heed of early evidence about scurvy and beriberi that pointed to the existence of vitamins, many deaths could have been avoided. As early as 1747, Dr. James Lind from Great Britain completed an experiment that showed that oranges and lemons prevented and cured scurvy. Yet for decades, no one paid any attention to this remarkably simple remedy. In 1882, Japanese navy doctor Kanehno Takaki showed that beriberi could also be cured with a few dietary changes. Takaki was concerned about the number of sailors Japan lost to beriberi. Noting the almost fanatical cleanliness of the Japanese navy, he could not see how beriberi could be a bacterial disease, especially when he saw that the less sanitary navies of other countries had no cases of the disease. Takaki concluded that beriberi must somehow be linked to diet.

Takaki set up an experiment in which he loaded one ship with the traditional Japanese navy diet, which relied heavily on rice, and packed another ship with a wider variety of provisions including fish, meat, vegetables, and milk. Following a nine-month voyage to South America, 169 of the 276 crew members on the traditional rice diet had fallen ill with beriberi, and 25 of them had died. There were only a handful of sick men on the other boat, and they confessed to having boycotted the "foreign" diet in favor of the

James Lind

traditional rice diet. These findings should have given medical researchers a clue to the nutritional nature of the disease, but instead most concluded that the men on the first ship had eaten contaminated rice.

With beriberi running rampant in the Dutch colonies in the 1880s, the Dutch were also trying to find a cure for the disease. The Netherlands sent medical officers to the East Indies to deal with the problem. Many guesses were made as to what caused beriberi, and everything from climate to fungi to spoiled fish was blamed. It was a time, however, when bacteria were being exposed as agents of disease, so it was only natural that the researchers focused their efforts on finding and combatting a beriberi-causing bacterium. One man claimed to have found the microorganism at last, but when chickens that the researchers were using as test animals were injected with the bacteria, nothing happened.

Eijkman and the Stingy Cook

As seems to have happened so often in medical mysteries, a chance occurrence opened the door to a cure for beriberi. Christiaan Eijkman, one of the Dutch medical officers on the island of Java, noticed that the chickens he was using in his research had developed a disease that was suspiciously like beriberi. Eijkman could find no evidence of bacteria or anything else that would explain the outbreak. Then, just as suddenly as it had come, the epidemic disappeared. Eijkman noticed that the change had happened at about the same time that the nearby hospital had changed cooks. The new cook was a stickler for saving money, and when he had discovered that the hospital had started providing expensive polished rice for Eijkman's chickens, he had put a stop to it. The change back to raw, unpolished rice seemed to have saved the chickens' lives.

Eijkman found the same connection between polished rice and beriberi at

Christiaan Eijkman

the island's jails. Natives of Java, who ate unpolished rice, had a low incidence of beriberi, while prisoners at the jail, who were fed polished rice, were dying in epidemic numbers from the disease. Eijkman concluded that there must be something in the rice bran, which is discarded during the polishing process, that was necessary for good health.

While most scientists scoffed at Eijkman's conclusions and continued to look to bacteria or poisoning for the cause of beriberi, the Dutch researcher's ideas received a favorable reception from British doctor Frederick Hopkins. It had been thought that all the body needs to survive are carbohydrates, protein, fat, minerals, and water, but the results of dietary experiments with mice had made Hopkins suspect that the body's nutritional needs were far more complex than had previously been guessed. Hopkins believed that there were other unknown elements necessary to life and that Eijkman had stumbled upon one of them in rice bran.

Vitamins

The skeptics, however, refused to believe that an "advancement" of technology, rice polishing, was actually a step backward, and they were not silenced until others had built upon the work of Eijkman and Hopkins. In 1911, a Polish researcher, Casimir Funk, studied Eijkman's reports and set out to find that mysterious ingredient in rice bran. From a starting mass of 831 pounds of unpolished rice, Funk was able to isolate 170

The chicken on the left was fed a normal diet, while the chicken on the right was fed a diet lacking in vitamins B and C. The vitamin deficiency has not only weakened the second bird, but it has also stunted its growth.

grams of a substance that prevented beriberi. The substance was a kind of chemical compound called an amine. Funk combined the word *amine* with *vita* the Latin word for "life," and called the life-giving substance a vitamine. The *e* was later dropped to create the word *vitamin*. Although Funk's chemical analysis did not turn out to be entirely correct, the name *vitamin* has been used ever since. The substance that eliminated beriberi turned out to be a vitamin called thiamine.

Two decades later, the Hungarian scientist Albert Szent-Györgyi was studying the function of the adrenal gland, which is located next to the kidney, when he found that the gland produced ascorbic acid, or vitamin C, a substance that prevents scurvy. At first, efforts to collect enough vitamin C to study proved nearly impossible. Several tons of animal adrenal glands yielded less than an ounce of the precious material. After years of frustration, Szent-Györgyi finally found another source of vitamin C in a plant that grew all around him: red peppers. This vegetable is used to make the famous Hungarian spice, paprika. From this vitamin storehouse, Szent-Györgyi was able to extract more than seven pounds of pure vitamin C, which made it possible for scientists to study the substance thoroughly and to eventually develop a way to produce it synthetically.

Eventually, more vitamins were discovered, analyzed, and artificially

Albert Szent-Györgyi

produced, and the evidence of their important roles was documented. Today, breakfast cereals, breads, juices, milk, and other foods are fortified with vitamins to help prevent a wide variety of health problems including rickets (a bone disease), pellagra (a skin disease), night blindness, and, of course, scurvy and beriberi. For their pioneering work in opening up this field of knowledge, Nobel Prizes for physiology or medicine were awarded to Christiaan Eijkman and Frederick Hopkins in 1929 and to Albert Szent-Györgyi in 1937.

Glossary

antibiotic — a substance produced by one microorganism that is harmful to another microorganism

antibody — a substance produced by the body that attacks disease-causing microorganisms

antitoxin — an antibody that protects the body against toxins

bacteria — the smallest one-celled organisms. Some bacteria are helpful, while others can cause dangerous diseases.

chemotherapy — the use of chemicals, or drugs, to treat disease

culture — microorganisms or cells grown in a material containing nutrients

flagella — whip-like structures found on certain organisms, such as the malaria protozoa, which help them to move

immune — able to resist disease

immunization — the process of using vaccines or serums to protect the body against disease

immunology — the study of immunity

insecticide — a substance used to kill insects

insulin — a substance produced by the islets of Langerhans in the pancreas that regulates the body's use of sugar

metabolize — to turn food into energy and cell "building blocks"

microbiology — the study of microorganisms

microorganisms — organisms too small to be seen by the naked eye, including bacteria, protozoa, and viruses

penicillin — an antibiotic used to treat infections caused by bacteria

protozoan — a one-celled animal that usually lives in water and can cause such diseases as malaria

serum — the liquid part of the blood that is left when the blood clots

sulfa drug — a chemical used to treat infections caused by bacteria

toxin — a poison produced by living organisms such as bacteria or viruses

tubercles — hard, grey lumps that form inside the bodies of tuberculosis victims when defending body cells surround tuberculosis bacteria

vaccination — the injection of a solution of disease-causing microorganisms to produce an immunity to that disease

vaccine — a solution of disease-causing microorganisms that stimulates the body to produce antibodies

virus — a microscopic organism without a cell structure of its own that lives in the cells of other organisms. Viruses are a major cause of disease.

Index

(Numbers in bold face refer to photographs)

ACKNOWLEDGMENTS:
The photographs in this book are reproduced through the courtesy of: pp. 6, 12, 17, 19, 20 (top), 23, 35, 37, 38, 46, 59, 67 (right), 69, 73, Library of Congress; pp. 9, 13, 22, 29, 34 (left), 34 (right), 41, 42 (left), 42 (right), 47, 48, 52, 58, 63, 67 (left), 72, 74, The Nobel Foundation; p. 11, University of Minnesota Archives; pp. 14, 16, 20 (bottom), 21, 24, 26, 28, 30, 32, 43, 49, 51, 54, 70 (bottom), 71, National Library of Medicine; pp. 15, 57, Centers for Disease Control, Atlanta, GA 30333; p. 39, American Medical Association; p. 40, Margaret Suckley, Franklin D. Roosevelt Library; p. 44, Wyeth Laboratories and the National Library of Medicine; p. 60, Dow Chemical Canada Inc.; p. 64, Eli Lilly and Company; p. 65, Banting and Best Department of Medical Research, University of Toronto; p. 66, Philadelphia Flyers; p. 70 (top), Independent Picture Service. Back cover photograph courtesy of the University of Minnesota Archives. Cover art by Mark Wilken.

ABOUT THE AUTHOR

Nathan Aaseng, who grew up in suburban Minneapolis, Minnesota, is a widely published author of books for young readers. He has explored far-ranging areas of interest, with college majors in English and biology, and work experience as a microbiologist/biochemist. Now a full-time writer, Aaseng has continued to delve into diverse subjects and has had more than 50 books published in the areas of sports strategy, biography, inspiration, and fiction. He now lives in Eau Claire, Wisconsin, with his wife and four children.